The
STORIES
Jesus Told

A BIBLE STUDY ON THE
PARABLES OF CHRIST

KAY GABRYSCH

WESTBOW
PRESS®
A DIVISION OF THOMAS NELSON
& ZONDERVAN

WestBow Press books may be ordered through booksellers or by contacting:

WestBow Press
A Division of Thomas Nelson & Zondervan
1663 Liberty Drive
Bloomington, IN 47403
www.westbowpress.com
844-714-3454

Scripture quotations are from the ESV® Bible (The Holy Bible, English Standard Version®), copyright © 2001 by Crossway, a publishing ministry of Good News Publishers. Used by permission. All rights reserved.

ISBN: 978-1-6642-5579-1 (sc)
ISBN: 978-1-6642-5580-7 (e)

Library of Congress Control Number: 2022901051

Print information available on the last page.

WestBow Press rev. date: 05/11/2022

Contents

• • • • •

Foreword

• • • • •

Welcome to a Bible study highlighting the very strategic storytelling of the Lord Jesus Christ. As Jesus spoke to the crowds, exhorted the religious leaders, and gathered his disciples, he utilized parables; stories with often hidden meanings but intentional points, over one-third of the time. Often the parable was in response to an accusation made against him. Sometimes there was an explanation of the parable given to his disciples. But the purpose was always the same: to sift his audience. Always his intention was that those who "had ears to hear" his stories, those who were truly listening carefully and trying to understand his words, would reorient their lives, rearrange their priorities, and follow him as kingdom citizens. Jesus often taught the parables in what has been referred to as a "window/mirror" format.[1] As he began to tell the story, he was inviting his hearers to look out an imaginary window and watch the narrative unfold. As he further engaged his audience, drawing them more and more into the story, it was as if, at a crucial point, he held up a hypothetical mirror to compel these listeners to see *themselves*

---

[1]   Zack Eswine, *Communicating Jesus with an Apologetic Sensitivity*, Lecture 7: "Sage Apologetics: Direct and Indirect Speech," DMin 866 (June 3–7, 2019), Covenant Theological Seminary, St. Louis, Missouri.

in the narrative. He clicked on the zoom button, brought the situation into focus in his hearers' lives, and called for a response.

The kingdom Jesus was inaugurating would begin the restoration of the entirety of human life for its citizens. Those who became kingdom citizens would be Christians living in the midst of a culture that was opposed to kingdom values. Jesus never told stories for the sake of entertainment but with the intention of spiritually and morally forming those who would live well as his followers. With every story, he displayed for his listeners' assessment situations, events, and characters who were either praiseworthy or blameworthy. In the parable of the Good Samaritan, for example, the Samaritan's actions were completely inconsistent with those of the religious leaders in the story, who had willfully ignored an individual in desperate need. In the Samaritan, Jesus painted a comprehensive, visibly contrasting picture of a man who *knew* that he was called to function in the world *for the sake of* the world, who was called *to love his neighbor as himself.*

Jesus told stories because human beings are storied people. We all live out of the story about God, ourselves, and his purposes for his world that we have told ourselves. Jesus invited his listeners to place themselves inside the Bible's story, never the other way around. His desire was for those who followed him to understand that they would be committing themselves to the responsibility of living as kingdom citizens, according to the King's purposes and under his authority.

As you read, study, and thoughtfully answer the questions on each parable, look for the unexpected truths Jesus is proclaiming as he invites his hearers to fit themselves into the Bible's kingdom story. Be aware of the ways in which he is pushing against the cultural and religious corruptions of his time. As an attentive reader, be alert to all the ways Jesus is teaching that the kingdom of God, which has come in him, is completely antithetical to the world, its ways, and the Jewish expectations of that time. As you spend time studying the stirring stories that the Lord Jesus told, pray that you will be one whose perceptions and directions are changed so that you think and act in accordance with the King. For the King, Jesus of Nazareth, has promised that "Blessed are your eyes, for they see, and your ears, for they hear" (Matthew 13:16). May that blessedness be yours as you open the parables and see the King in all his beauty.

Lesson 1

Introductory Lesson

• • • • •

When a child climbs up onto a parent's lap with a book in tow, he or she never says, "Will you tell me some *facts* about this, please?" Instead, a child will ask, "Will you read me a story?" From the earliest age, human beings are entertained, involved, and motivated by stories. When we open the pages of the New Testament, we find that the authors of the synoptic gospels present Jesus as the consummate storyteller. Jesus spent approximately one-third of his time in ministry creating stories that invited his listeners into a world where his message explained the kingdom of God, demonstrated the character of God, and challenged his hearers to redirect their lives in order to live happily in that kingdom. Although Jesus was often very direct in his assessment of those around him, it was his use of *indirect* speech in parables that seemed to have a more alluring, engaging effect on his audience.

The parables enabled Jesus's hearers to envision themselves inside the experience of the people involved in the story. It allowed them to insert themselves into the narrative and imagine what they might have done in that same situation. Jesus is the only person in the New Testament to tell parables, and he used them to bring people to a level of sober judgment about themselves and invite them to consider what it looks like to live in the kingdom Jesus was inaugurating. Jesus's parables were effective because they caught his hearers off guard, allowing them to drop their defenses in a way that direct speech does not. Klyne Snodgrass, a leading scholar on Jesus's parables, puts it like this:

> The immediate aim of a parable is to be compellingly interesting, and in being interesting it diverts attention and disarms … They are used by those who are trying to get God's people to stop, reconsider their ways, and change their behavior. Biblical parables reveal the kind of God that God is and how God acts and they show what humanity is and what humanity should and may become.[2]

Many of the parables end with the exhortation, "He who has ears to hear, let him hear!" It was Jesus's way of putting the responsibility on his listeners to respond to his teaching. The parables required not just acknowledgment but action.

---

[2]   Klyne Snodgrass, *Stories with Intent: A Comprehensive Guide to the Parables of Jesus*, Second edition (Grand Rapids, Michigan: William B. Eerdmans Publishing Company, 2018), 8–9.

How to Best Use This Study

This Bible study is best used as a twelve-week study with this introductory lesson as the first week's material and then the eleven subsequent studies each week after that. Each study after this first one will have specific questions pertinent to the particular parable it covers. There are many unique and wonderful parables Jesus told that have not been included in this study. For this reason, this first lesson contains general questions that can be used as a guide to study any of the parables. To start learning how to interpret the parables, choose any one of them, perhaps your favorite one, in the synoptic gospel accounts and consider the following questions:

1. Context:

    a. What is the setting for Jesus's telling of the story?

    b. To whom is he directing the story?

    c. To what question or situation is Jesus responding?

    d. What is the response of the audience to his story?

2. Once we have determined the context, we must listen for Jesus's communicative intent. One principle for interpretation of parables is called "the criterion of proportion." This means that the more central to the story something is, the more likely it is that it is indeed a symbol of what Jesus is emphasizing. One of the keys in interpretation of parables is to understand the great *significance* of some elements and the *limits* of others. Some elements of a parable are just used for effect but have no theological information. For example, the pigs in the story of the prodigal son are not to be assigned meaning that they simply don't have. Caring for them represents the bottom of the barrel for a young Jewish man because pigs were considered unclean animals. The fact that he is doing so demonstrates how far he has fallen, but other than that, there is no theological significance. If elements like pigs do not hold a central

place in the story, it is up to the reader to find out what does!

a. What preconceived ideas did you have about certain elements of the story you chose that need to be refocused to what matters most?

b. What or who is the most significant feature(s) or character(s) of his story?

c. Of what or of whom might that feature or character be a symbol?

3. Continuing on with the theme of Jesus's *intention* in telling the story, we can attempt to discern the theological significances. Jesus wants to convince his

listeners of specific aspects of God and his kingdom and humankind's response to this God and his purposes. Commenting on the theological significance of the parables, Snodgrass says, "The parables are a different kind of theological argument from what one finds in Romans, but they are just as theologically relevant."[3] Not all these questions will be answered in every parable.

a. What is revealed in the story about the *character* of God?

b. What is revealed about the *purposes* of God?

---

[3]   Snodgrass, 30.

c. What is revealed about different realities of life for people *in* or *out* of the kingdom of God?

d. What are some of your own ways of thinking or behaving that the parable causes you to stop and reconsider?

4. The biggest impact of each parable is always at the end of the story. Even in the shortest parables, the biggest indicator of Jesus's intent will be found at the conclusion. As you listen to Jesus's closing words, what impact or new thought do they leave with you?

The Parable of the Sower

• • • • •

Carefully read Matthew 13:1–23.

The parable of the sower is given a priority of place in all three synoptic gospels, and in Matthew, it is placed at the beginning of a lengthy eight-parable segment of Jesus's teaching about the kingdom of God. The parable is an explanation of why some people believe and some do not. It is designed to show the distinction between the believing heart and the hard, unbelieving heart. Although the gospel call of the Word of God is extended to all, it does not always fall on receptive hearts. Jesus is teaching the fundamental truth that those who hear it, who take it into their hearts and are changed by it will be the ones who enter the kingdom of God. He is simultaneously acknowledging that there will be those who will not receive it and will not enter the kingdom. The focus here is on the arrival of the kingdom of God by the power of the Word of God. The parable begs the question of what the response to that kingdom will be.

1. In Jesus's parables, he uses examples from everyday life to which his hearers could relate. In this agrarian society in first-century Palestine, the crowds would have been very familiar with a sower scattering his seed in hopes of attaining a crop. In the parable, the *same* seed is sown on four different types of soil. The first soil is representative of a hard heart into which the seed does not even penetrate (note the birds do not have to dig it out [v. 4]).

   a. What is Jesus's explanation in verse 19 for what happens with the first type of soil, and what might be a specific characteristic of that kind of heart attitude toward God's Word?

   b. The second soil is rocky with only a thin layer of soil. The seed "springs up" quickly but with no deep roots to sustain and nourish it. According to verses 20–21, what are the characteristics of that heart's *initial* reception of the Word of God, and why is that initial response not the guarantee of a true conversion?

According to John 16:1 and 16:33, what *is* the promise of Jesus to the persecuted one who *does* persevere with him?

c. The third soil was infested with thorns that choked the seed and kept it from bearing fruit. In verse 22, Jesus compares the stifling thorns with "cares of the world and deceitfulness of riches." What are some ways money or materialism causes anxiety in our daily decisions regarding security, stability, or consumption?

d. Although all four soils, or hearts, heard the same Word of God, only the last soil bore fruit. Only the last heart was penetrated, ruled, and transformed by the Word; *only the last heart* was the heart of a *true believer.* The story does not say that the good soil won't *ever* have rocks or thorns or cares; it just says they will not prevail. According to Matthew 13:23, James 1:21–25, and John 14:23, what will be the prevalent characteristics and comfort in the life of the true believer?

2. This is not a parable about four types of Christians. It is a parable about three types of *non-Christian* hearts and the one heart of a true believer. The dividing line is between *any response that falls short* of true life commitment to Jesus and the true commitment of the transformed life.

a. What then is Jesus clarifying about a person who has made a profession of faith, prayed a prayer, or walked an aisle but in whom there has been absolutely no life change nor any interest in the kingdom of God?

b. The parable makes it clear that there can be a "vast difference in our *confessional* beliefs and our *convictional* beliefs, those that are reflected in our actions."[4] It is not just our hearing and confessing but our *understanding* and *love* for Jesus and his words that will penetrate our hearts and shape our actions in everything in life. What are some areas of our lives we might need to examine to see where we may be willing to listen to him but unwilling to respond in obedience? (For help in thinking about this, see Matthew 5:1–11, where Jesus describes characteristics of kingdom citizens.)

3. By quoting the ancient Isaiah passage, Jesus is demonstrating that there has *always* been stubborn resistance to the Word of God. He warns the people listening to his parables that they are no different from the people of Isaiah's day. The emphasis here is on the *responsibility* of those in all ages who hear the Word of God.

---

4   Steve Wilkens and Mark L. Sanford, *Hidden Worldviews: Eight Cultural Stories that Shape Our Lives* (Downers Grove, Ill: IVP Academic, 2009), 22.

a. What is the oft-repeated key word in Matthew 13:13–15, 19, 23, and 51 that describes this responsibility of moving beyond just the surface of what is being said and taking it to heart?

b. Jesus adopted the use of parables at this stage of his ministry for the deliberate purpose of revealing more truth to those who had shown an interest in his Word. He is not asking for a theological understanding of every word he has said. What is the promise of Matthew 13:12, and how have you seen that promise realized in your own life as you put forth the effort to understand God's Word and battle competing ideas that come against it?

4. These parables are a picture of what God was actively doing through Jesus at that particular moment in redemptive history as he ushered in his kingdom. Matthew has purposely placed the parable of the sower and its seven accompanying parables in between two

accounts of two very specific historical events in order to make an important point.

Read the two accounts with which Matthew chose to bookend, or frame, the account of these eight kingdom parables. Those two bookends are found in Matthew 12:46–50 and Matthew 13:53–58.

a. By arranging the material in this way, what message is Matthew conveying to his Jewish audience about who will enter the kingdom?

b. How do these two events demonstrate how easily people can undervalue or even completely miss the new and beautiful aspects of God's transcendent kingdom activity when they are solely focused on the horizontal, imminent things going on around them?

5. The teaching of Jesus's parables *always* intersects with his nonparabolic teaching elsewhere in the gospels. A good principle is that if we have interpreted a parable to mean something that *cannot* be found elsewhere in Jesus's teaching, then we have interpreted it incorrectly. In each of the following passages, what is the direct teaching of Jesus that helps us to correctly discern Jesus's message in the parable?

a. John 8:43

b. Matthew 7:21–23

c. Matthew 12:49–50

Closing Thoughts

Matthew's message to a Jewish audience was "One greater than Isaiah is here," one who is not just the greater prophet but also the King who invites participation in his kingdom. That message must always be received, not with a casual or temporary encounter but with an all-encompassing embrace that leads to life-defining fruitfulness. True faith is *always* confirmed by a life of true discipleship, one that follows and delights in our great Prophet who proclaims his own life-changing Word.

The Pharisee and the Tax Collector

• • • • •

Carefully read Luke 18:9–14.

This parable is one of two in Luke 18 that deal with the hearts of praying people and the nature of the God whom they approach in prayer. The parable of the Pharisee and the tax collector is not a parable about prayer itself but rather a warning against pride and self-exaltation. It ends with a sense of impending judgment upon a person who self-righteously presumes upon the grace of God. The parable addresses the age-old question of what it is that establishes that a person is justified, declared to be in a right relationship with God. Jesus's verdict on that issue will be a startling one for his Jewish listeners.

1. Of the many parables Jesus taught, there are only three that contain an introductory statement revealing his actual intention in the teaching. In 18:9, the implication of the purpose statement is that this story will contain

a strong corrective. What does the introductory statement tell us about the connection between our *self-assessment* and our treatment of others?

2. By presenting a contrast of the thoughts, words, and actions of two praying men who are polar opposites, Jesus aims to bring about a surprising reversal in the conventional thinking of the day. It is important that we understand that Pharisees were highly respected among the Jews. Because they had studied and codified the law, Pharisees were considered to be the source of teachings on how to live righteously by the Jews who loyally looked to them for guidance.

a. Read Deuteronomy 26:16–19. This passage would have been part of the standard by which the Jews listening to Jesus would have measured the Pharisee's behavior and found it unobjectionable. However, upon careful observation, what are some noticeable differences between the *ideals* of the

Deuteronomy passage and this particular Pharisee's attitude and words?

b. The Pharisee does not acknowledge, nor does he even see a need for the grace of God. He congratulates himself on his external piety, which gives him a false assurance of his right to stand before a holy God. In Matthew 23, in a lengthy diatribe, Jesus expresses his own opinion of the hypocrisy of this kind of absurd commitment to *external* religiosity. Read Matthew 23:23–33. List some of the hypocritical behavior of the Pharisees and the ways in which Jesus sees it as an actual obstacle to true faith.

c. Legalism and self-righteousness are always enemies of the gospel of grace. What are some of the external behaviors or avoidances for which we create mental checklists for ourselves, our friends, or our children in order to self-justify or tell ourselves we are doing well in the eyes of God? How might our self-justification be an obstacle to seeing our need of God's grace in a particular area in which we think we are performing really well?

3. An all-important error in this Pharisee's thinking begins with the delusion that he can love God while despising all the people he has categorized as "not like him."

   a. According to Jesus's frequent emphases in Luke 10:25–37, Matthew 19:16–22, Matthew 22:34–39, and elsewhere, what would be the most consistent characteristics of a person who actually does love God?

   b. We hear so much these days about how polarized even Christians are in their strongly held beliefs. Those with whom we disagree are not just disdained;

they are demonized. How *should* Christians who are committed to following Jesus with their whole lives be engaging in ways that demonstrate the character of Christ to those whom we deem "not like us"?

c. What other preconceived wrong assumptions about God—that we may share—are evidenced by the Pharisee's words?

4. Because Jewish tax collectors had contracted with Rome to collect taxes from the Jews, they were considered traitors and held in great contempt. Jesus now turns from the well-respected Pharisee, who has no awareness of his own wickedness, to the man whose poignant plea displays his acute consciousness of his own sins.

a. What are the four noticeable expressions of the tax collector's self-awareness and need?

b. What does this reveal about what the tax collector knew to be true about God and true about himself?

5. The tax collector borrows his brief but powerful plea from the opening words of King David's great psalm of repentance, written after he had committed adultery and murder.

a. Read Psalm 51:1–10. What are all the actions God must undertake in order for David to be made right with God, and what must David do?

b. What does David inherently understand about the *heart* of a man who would carry out these abhorrent acts?

c. The verb "justified" in Jesus's parable is legal language that means "shown to be in the right, or acquitted." In the parable, the verb "justified" and the verb "exalted" are divine passive verbs that point to God as the actor. Jesus has contrasted the self-reliant Pharisaical heart, which refuses to acknowledge a need for the mercy of God, with the heart who humbly bows in recognition that there is no other hope. A dominant component of the gospel is the merciful compassion we see in this parable. The parable does not show us the tax collector's life *after* "he went home justified," but God assured the early church, through the New Testament writers, what was now true of *every* justified person.

Read Paul's assurance and promises to the church in Ephesians 2:4–9 and Titus 3:4–7. What do we learn about God's mercy and compassion for us? Will you ask God to help you recognize this kindness in your life? Will you let what He has done and is doing for you strengthen and uphold you this week?

Closing Thoughts

The gospel is about the greatest work of mercy ever done, the foundational work of mercy accomplished for us by Christ on the cross. Whenever a human being cries out for that mercy, it is always answered with a resounding "Yes!" from our God. Jesus's parable has an unexpected ending for those listeners who mistakenly thought that it was the Pharisee who was in good standing with God. The basis of the tax collector's acquittal is the recognition of his need and the compassion of a God who forgives sinners who throw themselves on his mercy.

In his timeless hymn "Rock of Ages," August Toplady describes the only way in which any human being can, in Jesus's words, "go down to his house justified."

Not the labor of my hands;
Can fulfill Thy law's demands;
Could my zeal no respite know,

Could my tears forever flow;
All for sin could not atone;
Thou must save, and Thou, alone.

Nothing in my hands I bring;
Simply to your cross I cling;
Naked come to you for dress;
Helpless look to you for grace;
Foul, I to the fountain fly;
Wash me, Savior, or I die.[5]

---

[5] August Toplady, *Rock of Ages, Trinity Hymnal*, (Atlanta, Georgia:Great Commission Publications, Inc.,2008), 499.

The Good Samaritan

• • • • •

Carefully read Luke 10:25–37.

In every parable, Jesus was asking his listeners to imagine a kingdom life that was verifiably different from the idolatrous communal life they had created for themselves. He taught that the kingdom would be present wherever the rule and reign of God was recognized, the power of God was experienced, and last but certainly not least, the *ethic* of God was embodied. Jesus stressed the *ethics* of the kingdom, not "works-righteousness," not earning salvation by good deeds, but what the practices would be of a community that was truly missional in love of neighbor. So, when the lawyer asks Jesus what he must "do" to have eternal life, Jesus essentially responds, "You're asking the wrong question; the issue is actually what is your relationship to God? Are your *practices* evidence of your love for God?" Jesus is outlining a way of life for Israel that demonstrates the full intent of the law.

Keep in mind as you read that the Jews lived in a very "tribalistic" world, one which excluded association with "outsiders." As Simon J. Kistemaker says, "The lines were carefully drawn to ensure the well-being of those who were inside and to deny help to those who were outside."[6] In the Jewish community, kinship, law, religion, and nationalistic pride had become elevated to the status of absolute good. It was an idolatry that Jesus consistently challenged in the parables.

1. While Jesus was teaching, a lawyer in the crowd asked him a common question.

   a. What is the question, and what does Jesus intend to establish by specifically asking him, "What does the law say, and how do *you* read it?"

   b. Read Deuteronomy 6:4–6. The answer that the lawyer (scribes who were experts in the law) gives to Jesus's question is at the very heart of Judaism. The proclamation is called the Shema and was to be recited twice a day by every Jewish male. The

---

6   Simon Kistemaker, *The Parables: Understanding the Stories Jesus Told*, New paperback ed. (Grand Rapids, MI: Baker Books, 2002), 141.

visible proof that one did indeed love the Lord as claimed was that he loved his neighbor as himself.

Read Leviticus 19:9–18.

What are all the actions the Lord commands here, and what choices could you make today to put any contemporary application of them into greater practice in your life?

c. Read Leviticus 19:33–34. How had the Lord clarified even further who the neighbor was who was to be loved, and what is the double rationale for this command?

2. The dissent that people had with Jesus over the love commands was never about the *importance* of the commands. They understood the commands' significance.

a. However, according to the following scriptures, what seems to be their struggle in carrying them out—Luke 10:29, Matthew 18:21, Luke 18:18–23?

b. Read Matthew 5:38–48. How does Jesus, for whom the love commands were central to his teaching, assess boundaries for acting on them?

3. Jesus tells the parable in order to rearrange the lawyer's thinking, to engage him in imagining God's true intention for kingdom life. The listeners are not told *why* the priest and the Levite saw the man and quickly went to the other side of the road without helping him, only that upon sight of him in his desperate condition, they did nothing to aid him. Because of the large influx of non-Jewish people into Israel, the question of who *qualified* as a neighbor was frequently asked. In the mind of any Jew, Samaritans would never have fallen into the category of neighbor; they had been natural enemies of the Jews since the days of the kings.

Everything that unfolds in the story would have been unanticipated for Jesus's listeners.

a. Read Matthew 7:12. Here, Jesus sums up the Law with a little variation but an interchangeable principle. No matter what the priest and Levite may have thought of the dangers involved or even the potential purity issues, if they had truly understood this principle of God's law, what should have been their governing ethic when they saw the man's dreadful plight? What actions have you taken this week in which Matthew 7:12 was your governing code, and what actions were counter to it?

b. What was the Samaritan's sentiment when he saw the man, and how is it a depiction of Jesus's own tenderness when he saw people in need, according to Matthew 9:36? What are some of our frequent biases when we look at those who are much less fortunate than us?

c. Jesus teaches that the long-awaited kingdom is now present with his coming. He proclaims that with the arrival of the kingdom, God has *now* begun acting in power to reverse evil and sin in the world and *restore* human life to its original *shalom*. What actions of the Samaritan exhibit this restoration in ways that are physical, economic, social, political, and so on?

4. The Lord is never ambiguous in describing his expectations of what biblical faith looks like in action. Peter Jones says that this parable "exposes any religion with a *mania* for creeds and an *anemia* for deeds."[7]

a. In the Old Testament, God emphasized specific deeds by which his people showed love to their neighbors. Israel's original calling was to be a missional people. They would live with each other, loving God and neighbor in such a way that they would be a light to the watching nations.

---

7   Peter Rhea Jones, *Studying the Parables of Jesus* (Macon, GA: Smyth & Helwys, 1999), 314 (italics mine).

Read Isaiah 58:3–12, and write down some of the many actions that God's people would take if they were loving their neighbor as themselves. What would have been God's assessment of his people if this had happened?

b. Once Jesus declares that the kingdom is now here, his mission is to begin forming the community about which Isaiah is actually prophesying, the one that will carry on where Israel failed. God's role for his people has never changed. What would be God's assessment of his church, and what kind of attraction would it be to the unbelieving world today if the church of Jesus Christ was living in this missional way?

c. Secular culture is often characterized by a lack of love of neighbor. How can we fight against the human tendencies by which this attitude infiltrates the church?

5. Parables do not give the church or individual Christians specifics regarding *how* to love a neighbor in any given situation. But we *are* given the wisdom of all of Scripture to determine the path to take in a particular circumstance that will best express our love for God. What the parable does teach clearly is that our relationship with God is expressed through our relations with our neighbors, and there is no such thing as an image bearer of God who is a nonneighbor.

As you study this parable, how is God challenging your passivity in regard to loving those whom you consider nonneighbors in an active, merciful way *because* you are a follower of Jesus?

Closing Thoughts

Jesus challenged his hearers to see that if they truly loved God with all their heart, soul, mind, and strength, they would remove any limits on their obligations to love their neighbor. Kingdom life would be lived in such conformity to Christ that it would exhibit radical kindness and complete unselfishness in every encounter with fellow image bearers of God. Kingdom citizens would extend compassion and love across well-defined boundaries of exclusion. It is only by living in this way that the church of the Lord Jesus Christ can fulfill her calling to be a light to the unbelieving world. When it lives in this way, the church will be the sign to all the world of what life will look like when evil is conquered and true humanity is restored.

Lesson 5

The Rich Fool

• • • • •

Carefully read Luke 12:13–21.

There is probably no message in any of Jesus's parables that is as contradictory to the thinking of modern western Christians as this one. When it comes to material possessions, we tend to reason more like Tevye in *Fiddler on the Roof*, who, when he was told that money was the world's worst curse, responded, "May the Lord smite me with it, and may I never recover!" In chapter 12 of Luke's gospel, Jesus had been teaching his disciples about faithfulness in situations of persecution when he was abruptly confronted by a man in the crowd who was clearly not interested in the topic. The disruptive man had a domestic matter on his mind with which he boldly sought Jesus's assistance. "Teacher," he shouts, "tell my brother to divide the inheritance with me." Undeterred, Jesus returns to his subject of fidelity in discipleship, developing a fresh focus, that of faithfulness with one's possessions.

1. Jesus is issuing a strong warning about guarding one's heart against covetousness, the overwhelming desire to have what God has not given.

    a. If the crowd was inclined to be empathetic to the man's demand, how did Jesus *immediately* censure that idea?

    b. Read James 4:1–4. What are the utter condemnations James issues for what is apparently going on in this man's life?

    c. When Jesus uses the word *life*, he is talking about an orientation of the whole of life toward consumerism. Some aspects of consumerism are thinking that every problem can be solved by possessions or resources or that accumulating things brings fulfilment. What are some of the ways the culture leads people to believe that fulfilment is found in wealth and everything that comes with it?

2. It is important to remember that Jesus came to renew and restore his people and his creation. His reconstitution of Israel meant reorienting them to the purposes God had always intended for them. From the beginning of Israel's history, God had been very explicit regarding how his people were to handle their resources.

   a. Read carefully Leviticus 23:22 and 25:15, 18–23, 28,35. What are some of the ways in which the Israelites were to use their possessions?

   b. Read Leviticus 26:3–5, 9–12. What would be the beneficent results of the people of God living in this way?

c. By commanding these practices in regard to their possessions, what was the deeper truth the Lord was teaching them, and how is this mindset reiterated for God's renewed people in 1 Timothy 6:17–19?

3. The Lord calls the rich man in the parable a fool! Read Proverbs 28:26 and Proverbs 3:5–6.

a. The man has undeniably demonstrated his greed. But something else is implicit in Jesus's story. According to Proverbs, what is the fundamental reason for the Lord's condemnation of the man as a fool?

b. Read Matthew 6:24. How does the story of the rich fool illustrate this proclamation of Jesus?

4. In the parable, Jesus has told the story of a fool who lived in the moment, trusting in his own resources with no understanding of the inadequacy or fragility of that in which he had trusted. In the discourse that follows the parable, Jesus pivots, lifting his hearers up from the mire of the fool's life into the transcendence of the character and activity of God.

   a. In verses 21–34, what does Jesus warn will consume a person's heart and mind when money and security have primacy of place?

   b. Jesus knows that the actions he has been condemning are grounded in a faulty understanding of the character of God. He reorients their misguided ideas by pointing to God's observable care for his creation.

Read Psalm 8. Of what would Jesus's Jewish listeners, familiar with this psalm, have been reminded when Jesus began to compare God's care for creation with his care for mankind?

c. What are some of the truths of Psalm 8 and this passage that remind you of your value and worth to your Heavenly Father and help you to trust him more because he loves you so?

5. The *cure* for the false reliance on possessions is also given in the discourse of verses 21–34. Jesus is teaching his listeners to understand God's love for them by observing the presence of God all around them. By lifting their eyes to his character, God is teaching them to trust Him instead of their own concerns for self-security.

a. When Jesus exhorts his hearers to "seek first the kingdom," he means the completely new way of life that he is ushering in by his presence, one that is antithetical to the ways in which the world measures wealth and power. To seek is to pursue. In the power of the Holy Spirit, what decisions can you make this week to *stop* pursuing things that are destroying your peace?

b. Read Matthew 19:16–22, one of Jesus's most important teachings on how a love of money can claim a life.

When we read this story, we wonder, *Is Jesus this demanding of everybody? Does he really expect these kinds of drastic actions?* The short answer is yes.

Coming to maturity in Christ will always involve divesting ourselves of the idols that hold sway over our hearts. What is the entryway to the "treasure in heaven" that Jesus gives the rich young man at the end of verse 21, and what might he be asking you to do to walk further through that door?

c. Jesus sums up the parable of the rich fool and the teaching of the discourse with Luke 12:34. Read it along with Colossians 3:1–4. How is Paul further developing Jesus's teaching, and how have all of these passages encouraged you today regarding your security?

Closing Thoughts

In the parable of the rich fool and the discourse that followed it, Jesus has impressed upon his disciples that a life completely oriented to God and his kingdom will be free of anxiety and worry in every earthly sphere, especially concerning one's resources. That happens when every good thing is put down to its rightful place, and hearts and minds are set on the One who rules his kingdom from above. May we experience and enjoy the gifts of this world but do so without being enchanted by them, living in continuous acknowledgment that only the Lord is proportional to our true needs; only he is the ultimate joy of every longing heart.

Lesson 6

The Lost Sheep

● ● ● ● ●

Carefully read Matthew 18:12–14 and Luke 15:1–7.

Because this parable appears to be set in two different contexts by the two different gospel writers, it is possible that Jesus told it on more than one occasion. Stories about shepherds and sheep were quite common in this agrarian culture. However, it is always important to remember that each of the gospel writers has a different point of emphasis when he tells the stories of his or his source's memories of Jesus. Matthew's account prioritizes God's rescue of the "little ones," those who are already in the faith but who may be immature with a tendency to wander or "stray" from the fold. Luke highlights those who are "lost" and in need of the seeking and *saving* grace of God. In both accounts, the fundamental, enduring message is the same; it is God who not only takes the initiative to seek and save but also rejoices over each and every one of his own lost or straying sheep.

1. The principle audience in the Matthew narrative is discovered in 18:1–6.

   a. Who is Jesus primarily teaching here, and what is it that he wants them to know about themselves and their discipleship of others?

   b. Matthew is concerned throughout his gospel to demonstrate Jesus's training of the disciples so that they become men who will lead his church in his way and with his priorities. According to the following verses, what were some of his high expectations of them, and how are these instructions being put into practice in your life?

   Matthew 9:36–38

Matthew 28:18–20

c. The parable doesn't address the question of whether the straying sheep *deserves* to be rescued or the amount of effort required to disentangle it from the trouble that very well could have been self-inflicted. It only assures the listener that the rescue is a cause of the shepherd's rejoicing. What are some ways Jesus might be calling you to imitate him in this rescue effort of others right now?

2. In the Matthew parable, the shepherd leaves the ninety-nine sheep in someone else's care in order to prioritize the one sheep that has gone astray.

    a. What does Jesus say in verse 14 is the reason for this prioritizing?

    b. Read John 10:27–30. How does Jesus's teaching in this passage reinforce and enhance the teaching of verse 14 of the parable?

3. We turn now to Luke's account of the parable, where Jesus's critics are very troubled by his inclusiveness, particularly at meals, long considered a time of intimate fellowship. Jesus, however, considered each meal with the social and moral outcast to be the setting for a divine encounter.

    a. In his book *Contagious Holiness*, Craig L. Blomberg questions whether Jesus was the "ultimate party-animal." He comments on "Jesus's love of associating with a broad cross-section of people, but particularly the outcasts of Jewish society in the context of festive banquets."[8] Read Matthew 9:9–13. What is Jesus's own explanation of why he eats with the outcasts of society?

b. It is clear throughout the gospel accounts that Jesus's meals with sinners are both a fulfilment of prophecy and a forerunner of the great eschatological banquet in the New Creation. Read Isaiah 55:1–3. What is the prophecy promising that Jesus is delivering, and to whom is the invitation extended?

4. It is because of the religious leaders' failure to see the redemptive purposes in his table fellowship that Jesus will tell them the parable of the shepherd who goes after a lost sheep. He frames the parable on an Old Testament tradition with which they should have been very familiar, that of the shepherd and his responsibility

---

8   Craig L. Blomberg, *Contagious Holiness: Jesus' Meals with Sinners*, New Studies in Biblical Theology 19 (Leicester, England: Downers Grove, IL: Apollos, InterVarsity Press, 2005), 97.

for his sheep. Read the following passages in Ezekiel: Ezekiel 34:1–6, 11–16, 23–24.

a. What are the accusations of the Lord against the religious leaders?

b. Since the religious leaders are derelict in their duty, what initiatives does the Lord promise to take upon himself on behalf of the sheep?

c. In John 10:7–18, what are all the ways Jesus sees himself as the fulfilment of Ezekiel's promises?

5. Jesus's parable in Luke is focused on the certainty of the seeking and the celebration of the finding. His question to the religious leaders implies an argument

from the lesser to the greater. "What man of you wouldn't do this for one of your sheep?" he asks, the implication being that if you would do this for a sheep, how much more will the Lord go after a lost human being.

a. The emphasis of the parable is on God's limitless grace. However, there is a necessary requirement for the sinner—repentance. What is noteworthy about the order in which the seeking and repentance takes place?

b. The parable doesn't teach anything at all about the *nature* of repentance, only the *value* God places on it. How is this demonstrated, and what is it about the Lord's response that not only calls you to evangelism but also spurs you on to daily, even hourly, repentance in your own life?

6. Jesus's parables were designed to remind his listeners of the ways in which God had *always* dealt with his people. Read Zephaniah 3:16–19, written to God's people before they were carried away into exile in Babylon, scattered and separated from the Lord's presence because of their own sins. What are some of the ways he promises to deal with them when he rescues them, and what comfort do you get from these promises for your own life today?

Closing Thoughts

The grumbling religious leaders failed to see that by eating with outcasts, Jesus was carrying out the very activity God had promised through the prophets; He was pursuing the straying and lost sheep. Their assumptions about the character of God and His grace were completely deficient. These parables are a reminder of the infinite lengths to which God will go to rescue his own and to keep them in his care. We are reminded that God doesn't just seek those who are lost outside the family of God but that he also cares about the insignificant, marginalized people *within* the church. Jesus is asking us not only to understand the character of God but to emulate it, being Christians who seek out those who are in need of his grace, help them to experience it, and rejoice with them when they do.

The Prodigal Son

• • • • •

Read carefully Luke 15:11–32.

This is arguably the most well-known of Jesus's parables, depicted through the ages more than any other by great artists, most prominently Rembrandt, as well as in beautiful music and even Shakespearean plays. Luke groups the three stories of "lost-ness" together in chapter 15, the parables of the lost sheep, the lost coin, and the lost son, in order to make a point regarding God's celebration over the restoration of that which was lost but has been recovered. However, in the parable of the prodigal son, there are important variations and implications of that theme that teach much more about sin, self-righteousness, and salvation by grace than do the other parables in the trio. The setting for the parable of the prodigal son is the same as that of the lost sheep and the lost coin. Jesus is still addressing a mixed crowd of people, some of whom are outcasts of society and some who are religious leaders who are very concerned about Jesus's reception of these moral outcasts, especially his welcoming of them into table fellowship. It is important to keep this audience in mind as you read.

1. Jesus begins the parable by casting the presumptuous younger son in a disparaging light. The son's request would have been a disgraceful breach of family ties in this culture.

    a. Read Exodus 20:12. After God has given four commandments regarding his people's relationship to *him*, he turns to their relationship with *others*. This command has primacy of place in the last six, the requirements for "horizontal" relationships. What can be surmised about the heart attitude of the younger son toward the law of God by observing his behavior regarding this commandment?

b. Now read Luke 11:1–13 and 12:27–32. What are the some of the *unfamiliar* ideas about God as a Father that Jesus has already introduced, and how do they parallel this father's response in verse 12?

2. Jesus then relates a series of events in the younger son's rebellious life that distance him further and further from his family. Life for the son deteriorates to the point that the father later describes him in his alienated condition as "dead."

   a. What is included in the shameful chain of events that transpires, and what implicit contrast does Jesus draw to the son's former life in verse 16?

   b. According to Romans 2:4, what is it that leads a person to repentance, and how do you see that illustrated in both the son's thoughts about his father as he comes to his senses and the father's initial sentiment upon seeing his son?

c. The absurdity of a wealthy landowner running down the road to publicly receive a wayward son would have been an outlandish picture for the Pharisees to grasp. What more does the father do to demonstrate grace and honorable restoration of the son who had rejected him?

3. Jesus's parables confront his hearers with the narrowness of their thinking. The listening Pharisees would have deemed the boy in the story completely worthless because of his behavior; after all, the boy had identified *himself* as "no longer worthy to be called your son."

a. What is the joyous truth that the social and moral outcasts who were listening to the story would have heard from the father's own lips regarding the boy's worth and identity?

b. Since these things are gloriously true, what is the message of the parable to every person without Christ, and where might a disdainful disposition toward some be interfering with your delivery of this good news? Are there some, in your opinion, who do not deserve this kind of treatment, and if so, why?

4. Jesus now reintroduces the elder brother into the story, painting the picture of a young man with a disdainful, condescending attitude who believes that *he* has upheld the standards of sonship.

a. How is the loving compassion of the father revealed again in his action toward the elder son, and what are the many sins recognizably flowing from the son's heart in his response to the father's love?

b. How is the elder son, who thinks he has nothing from which to repent, *also* breaking the Fifth Commandment, and what is it the son thinks he has done to earn what is "due" him?

c. How does the father refute the idea that the son has "earned" anything, and how does Jesus denounce the son's idea even further in Luke 17:7–10?

5. The son is so out of touch with what God is doing that he has nothing but disdain for the celebration of his brother's restoration. Those who have tried cheerlessly to earn their salvation do not recognize the joy that *must* accompany the celebration-warranting good news of the gospel. The Jews listening to Jesus would have

known well the story of the prophet Jonah, who was sent to the wicked and, in Jonah's opinion, undeserving Ninevites to preach repentance. Jesus teaches some of those same eternal truths in the parable.

a. Read Jonah 4, which picks up the story after God has forgiven the repentant Ninevites, whom Jonah held in great disdain. What are some parallels in the elder son's story with Jonah's story? (Pay particular attention to the questions God asks Jonah, and compare them to the words of the father in the parable.)

b. The unbelieving world often sees Christians as angry and mean-spirited. Think carefully about what might be some reasons for that perception, and write down your thoughts.

6. The Bible does not divide lost people into two camps of *good* lost people and *bad* lost people; Jesus makes it clear that *both* brothers were lost. The promises of God regarding salvation by grace have been based on what is true of *all* of God's image bearers. They are *all* rebellious, estranged creatures in need of the reconciliation to their heavenly Father that only he can provide. The following remarkable assurances are true of *all* who have received that reconciliation and restoration. Which of the glorious elements of the salvation that he has provided cause you personally to rejoice the most and why?

   a. Ephesians 1:3–14

   b. Hebrews 2:10–13

Closing Thoughts

There is a cohesive thread running through the parables of Luke 15 in which Jesus teaches the divine necessity of joy over the restoration of the lost. In this particular parable, there is a reason for that kingdom joy that Jesus longed for his hearers to grasp. Sinclair Ferguson, in his excellent book *Children of the Living God*, says this: "Bringing us into his family is the work of the triune God in all his glory. The Father destines us to be his children; the Son comes to make us his brothers and sisters; the Spirit is sent as the Spirit of adoption to make us fully aware of our privileges ..."[9]

All of our attitudes and obedience should stem from a *celebration* of the fact that we are dearly beloved children who can come home to the Father with our self-inflicted wounds and be forgiven and reconciled to him because of the gracious and faithful action of our true Elder Brother. J. I. Packer says that our grasping of this truth makes all the difference in how we actually live the Christian life: "If you want to judge how well a person understands Christianity, find out how much he makes of the thought of being God's child, and having God as his Father."[10] The Father has invited us to the celebration of our restoration that his Son's victory achieved; it is a cause for extravagant rejoicing.

---

[9]   Sinclair Ferguson, *Children of the Living God* (Carlisle, PA: Banner of Truth Trust, 1989), 4–5.

[10]   J. I. Packer, *Knowing God* (London: Hodder and Stoughton, 1973), 182.

The Ten Virgins

• • • • •

Read carefully Matthew 25:1–13.

The parables of Matthew 24–25 have a sharp focus on future judgment. Jesus is prophetically orienting his listeners to what will happen when the Lord comes in judgment to separate the unbelieving world from those who will live with him in eternal bliss. Instead of beginning this parable with his usual present tense introduction of "The kingdom of heaven *is* like …," he starts with "*Then* the kingdom of heaven *will be* like …" locating his kingdom story in the future. In the judgment parables, there is always a distinction drawn between two different kinds of people. In this story, Jesus emphasizes the contrasting moral and intellectual characteristics that are attributed to those who will be with Jesus and those who will not.

1. Throughout the judgment parables, there are false assumptions made regarding the timing of the coming of the Lord. The inaccurate idea that the bridegroom was

coming *soon* is implied by the fact that the foolish virgins thought there would be no need for extra provisions.

a. Contrast that attitude with the equally incorrect expectation of Matthew 24:48–51?

b. According to Matthew 24:36, what had Jesus clearly taught regarding that timing?

c. What might be some reasons people are so inclined to look for Jesus's second coming behind every current event, and how does that undermine what Jesus has so plainly said?

2. In the gospels, the Christian life is painted as a life of joy-filled demands and rigorous discipleship. What is the one thread running through all of the following scriptures?

Luke 12:35–40

Luke 21:34–36

Mark 13:34–37

3. The Bible is replete with vivid portraits of both foolishness and wisdom. Because Jesus says both are represented in this parable, we will look at some biblical descriptions of both.

a. What characteristics of wisdom or foolishness are spoken of in each of the following passages. Explore each scripture to see the many different facets of the wise or foolish person.

James 3:13–17

Proverbs 14:15

Proverbs 18:2

Proverbs 26:11

Ecclesiastes 7:9

b. As followers of Jesus, we must be able to say biblically that "x" is foolish and "y" is wise and then refuse to give our hearts and minds to foolish thinking and behavior. How do the preceding passages both convict and encourage you to carefully test your thoughts and actions by God's word this very day?

4. It is not the sleeping that is condemned in the parable; even the *wise* virgins fall asleep when the bridegroom is delayed.

a. What is it that *is* being denounced regarding the foolish women?

b. In our human nature, we might think that it is rather selfish of the wise virgins not to share their oil. Why, on the contrary, would this not have been a good plan, and how do you see the foolish virgins' inability to see that they have done anything wrong displayed?

c. The shut door is not just a missed opportunity. Jesus is giving the radical warning that those who have not lived in wisdom and readiness are not prepared for his coming reign on earth and will be excluded from it. The readiness Jesus is asking for is "… an attitude, a commitment, and a lifestyle."[11] What are some of the ways you are taking seriously the promise of God and practicing readiness for Christ's coming in your own lifestyle? How does this parable encourage you to persevere?

---

[11]   Snodgrass, *Stories with Intent*, 518.

5. The biblical pattern throughout the entire narrative of Scripture is that God's people have always been waiting for him. The Bible's *question* for God's people has always been what manner of life will they lead as they wait?

   a. Read Luke 2:22–32. In what ways is Simeon a demonstration of the life lived in godly waiting and preparation for the Lord's advent?

   b. Read 2 Peter 3:1–4. What does Peter urge believers to do as they wait for the Lord's second coming, which was also the faithful practice of Simeon as he waited for the Messiah's first coming?

c. Considering what Peter says about the "scoffers," what are some "scoffer-like" thought patterns into which Christians can slip when they forget God's promises and engage in foolish speculations based on what is going on in the world?

Closing Thoughts

Jesus's followers live in expectation of that day when He returns to take his bride to himself, to live with her eternally here on this earth. The parable of the ten virgins reminds his listeners that Jesus, also, has expectations. He expects to find that his people have lived faithfully, in preparedness and readiness for his eternal reign. He expects to find that the church, like Simeon of old, has lived in the midst of turmoil and chaos with the unique perspective that only a complete trust in the promises of God brings.

The Unforgiving Servant

• • • • •

Carefully read Matthew 18:21–35.

Matthew records five lengthy sermons from Jesus; this fourth one is referred to by one of the church fathers as "The Sermon on the Congregation." All of chapter 18 is an ecclesiastical discourse in which Jesus is training his disciples regarding how they will live in relationship to others in the church, which will be the contrasting community of the kingdom. Because the church will be the vehicle by which God will expand his kingdom, the "great" citizens of that kingdom community must exhibit certain qualities. The disciples lived in a status-conscious world, but as Craig Keener says, "Status in the kingdom is often inversely proportional to status in the world."[12] Jesus's teaching throughout this chapter will emphasize that the great ones will be those who have learned how to deal compassionately and lovingly with *fellow sinners* within the community of God. Keep in mind as you study this

---

[12] Craig S. Keener, *A Commentary on the Gospel of Matthew* (Grand Rapids, MI: W. B. Eerdmans Pub, 1999), 447.

parable that Jesus tells this story as a warning. He is teaching that the person who has truly experienced the forgiving grace of God will stand righteous before the judgment of God.

1. Because the *context* of the parable of the unforgiving servant is so integral to its understanding, we will back up and read Matthew 18:1–20. When the disciples ask Jesus in Matthew 18:1 who will be the greatest in the *kingdom*, they are inviting a *royal* comparison. They are concerned with what their important royal roles will be when *they* are publicly aligned with this King.

   a. What stark contrast does Jesus then draw for them in verses 2–4 regarding who will actually be considered great?

   b. With what warning does Jesus then turn their focus away from themselves to the importance of their treatment of others and their own self-denial?

c. As the discourse continues in verse 15, Jesus moves into another sphere in which the Christian must put others first. How does Jesus emphasize yet again that it is the honor of the other person that must be given priority, and how do we often neglect that teaching when we have been wronged by another?

2. The parable of the unforgiving servant is climactically and strategically placed at the end of the sermon that is Matthew 18. The trajectory of Jesus's words from the beginning of the discourse led to the parable in verses 21–35, which comprise the *essence* of his teaching on the mercy and forgiveness that is the responsibility of a kingdom citizen.

a. Read again verses 21–22. Despite the weakness in Peter's question, he *doubles* the standard of the Jewish forgiveness requirement of three times and even adds one more for good measure! What does this demonstrate about Peter and his intentions now that he is a disciple of Jesus?

b. Read Genesis 4:23–24. Beginning with Adam and Eve's immediate descendants, revenge has been seen as an insignia of heroism to fallen mankind. What does Jesus, using the same language as the boastful Lamech, characterize as true heroism in a kingdom citizen?

c. How do Jesus's words help you assess how much you may be clinging to the "right" to unforgiveness, and what are some of the subtle ways by which we make that known to an offender?

3. In this parable, there are two settlings of legal accounts, one at the beginning and one at the end. Jesus is teaching the disciples that with the settling of the first

account on their behalf comes a responsibility to live in a certain way.

a. In order to make his points emphatically, Jesus highly exaggerates every detail of the story, including the astronomical sum of money that the servant owed to the king. The amount was more money than would have existed in the whole country. The first point about humanity Jesus is making is that we are infinitely in debt to God. What is the subsequent truth regarding that debt?

b. How does what the servant asked for compare to what the king actually gave him?

c. What is the *only* reason given for the king's forgiveness of the debt, and how does that expand your understanding of God's mercy in your own life?

4. In verse 28, the story pivots to the servant's response to what the king has just done. As Klyne Snodgrass comments, the ethic of the kingdom citizen must be "... responsive and reflective—*responding* to God's prior action and *reflecting* God's character."[13]

   a. The first servant went out and found a man who owed him the tiniest fraction of what the first servant had owed the king; one scholar estimates it as less than one-millionth. What is noticeable about the desperate pleas of both men in verses 26 *and* 29, and how does that highlight the contrast between the response to those pleas from both the king and the first servant?

---

[13] Snodgrass, *Stories with Intent*, 72 (italics mine).

b. Read Luke 7:36–47. Considering Jesus's instructive remarks to Simon the Pharisee in Luke 7:47, what is one conclusion we can reasonably draw regarding the parable's first servant's assessment of his own debt?

c. Additionally, what conclusion can we draw regarding his *appreciation* of the king's mercy to him?

5. F. D. Bruner concludes his commentary regarding the king's final actions with this statement: "… while the Lord's forgiving was without required conditions, it was not without expected consequences …"[14]

---

14 Frederick Dale Bruner, *Matthew: A Commentary Vol. 2* (Grand Rapids, MI: William B. Eerdmans, 2004), 240.

a. According to verse 33, what is the reason for the king's anger and subsequent judgment on the servant?

b. Read Psalm 103:2–4 and Colossians 3:12–17. What difference would it make in your actions toward others today if you kept these truths, along with this parable, uppermost in your mind?

c. How does Jesus's closing statement of accountability, especially his last three words, challenge us to take seriously the truth that true biblical grace must be transforming grace?

Closing Thoughts

It has been said, "When you get the gift you get the Giver, who will not let you go your own way."[15] Jesus consistently teaches that the person who has actually been converted by the grace of God will demonstrate evidence of a transformed life. This parable's main concern is the *responsibility* of the one who has received the grace and mercy of God to then mirror that same grace and mercy *to others*. "If God's mercy does not take root in the heart, it is not experienced. Forgiveness not shown is forgiveness not known."[16] Jesus's sermon reminds those of us who live in a hyperindividualistic culture that we have a responsibility for self-denial, not personal rights; mercy, not judgment; and forgiveness, not revenge. May the Lord enable us to see these things the way he sees them.

---

[15] Snodgrass, *Stories with Intent*, 75.
[16] Snodgrass, 75.

The Wise and Foolish Builders

• • • • •

Read carefully Matthew 7:24–27.

This parable, which concludes the Sermon on the Mount, is both a hopeful encouragement and a dire warning. The Sermon on the Mount is Jesus's lengthiest teaching on the descriptions and responsibilities of the serious Christian life. What Jesus is proclaiming throughout the sermon is not moralism or legalism but the necessity of a completely new way of life for those who would follow him. There is nothing about the discourse that encourages righteousness or good works apart from new birth in Christ. In fact, the more we read it, the more we understand that we *cannot* evidence these characteristics apart from divine enabling. There is a twofold purpose in Jesus's speech: to both paint a portrait of the true disciple and to create the true disciple. As Frederick Dale Bruner says, "To read the Sermon on the Mount is to discover what it *means* to be Jesus' disciples; to read it with (a heart of) faith is to receive power to *be* Jesus' disciples."[17] As we study the parable at the end of the sermon, we will look at some of what our Lord is actually commanding us to put into practice.

1. Contrasts are prevalent in the Sermon on the Mount. It was very common for Jesus to present two ways of *doing* things, the correct and incorrect way to pray, the proper and improper treasure to store up, the broad and narrow roads on which to walk, and many others.

   a. Write down the similar thoughts in the parable of the two builders and the teaching in Matthew 7:15–20.

   b. According to both of these passages, what are the obvious ways to identify a believer?

---

17 Frederick Dale Bruner, *Matthew: A Commentary Vol. 1* (Grand Rapids, MI: William B. Eerdmans, 2004), 151.

2. According to Jesus, there are *two* indispensable steps that validate a true believer, or the one he identifies as a wise person.

a. What are these two requirements in verse 24, and how does Jesus emphasize that identification even more strongly in Luke 8:19–21?

b. Read Matthew 21:28–31. According to Jesus's requirements, which of the sons is in the will of the Father, and why might he be telling this little story to the religious leaders?

c. What might be some specific areas of life where you are *agreeing* with what God's Word says but not *doing* anything about it?

3. In the upside-down kingdom of God about which Jesus is teaching in the Sermon on the Mount, true Christians will look, act, and actually *be* a certain way as they put Jesus's words into practice. When they do, He promises that they will be a light shining in the darkness, the faithful presence of Christ in the world.

Read through Matthew 5: 2–12.

What stands out to you in these descriptors that is antithetical to the behavior of many Christians today? Why are Christians often more interested in fighting and winning culture wars than they are in becoming who Jesus is characterizing here?

4. The bottom line for this parable is that whoever hears Jesus's words and puts them into practice is wise, and whoever does not is foolish.

In the following passages, what are the actual commands, and what would it look like for you to put them into practice in your own life?

a. Matthew 5:21–24

b. Matthew 5:43–48

c. Matthew 6:25–34

5. Jesus is unambiguous that this parable is about both blessing and cursing. Security will come from obedience but destruction from disobedience.

a. What is true of the storms that come against the two different houses?

b. In the first century, just as now, Jesus was speaking to many people who wanted to be "great" in the eyes of the world. Jesus's teaching is filled with a war against greatness. What is the irony of those who would choose that over being a disciple of Jesus?

c. Read John 15:4–11. What are all the ways stability and security will come to the Christian, and how does this fill you today with the joy that he has promised?

Closing Thoughts

In the Sermon on the Mount, Jesus is asking his listeners to imagine a community where people are not angry, do not lust, always tell the truth, and never retaliate with violence. He ends his sermon by assuring them that should they live this way, there will be peace and security in their lives even in the midst of the tribulation that will accompany discipleship. Frederick Bruner says, "Jesus does not say that a house built on his words will ... miraculously expand into a mansion, or in some other way become impressive. The only impressive thing about this house is that it will be standing when the storm is over."[18] The Christian has been invited by the Lord to build a life on the only foundation that will.

---

[18] Bruner, 359–360.

Lesson 11

The Talents

• • • • •

Read carefully Matthew 25:14–30

In the parable of the talents, Jesus is teaching about the interim period between His first and second comings. He is concerned with the question of the faithfulness of his servants during that interval. With Jesus's first advent, the kingdom has come, and all those who are citizens of it have been called by him to service in that kingdom. King Jesus will one day return to consummate his kingdom, to bring it in all its fullness, and when he does, he will ask for an accounting of what his servants have done with the grace with which they were entrusted.

1. The meaning we most commonly use for the word *talent*, which usually refers to human ability, originated with this parable. But a talent in antiquity was actually a monetary weight of a particular metal. The value of one talent was equivalent to six thousand days' wages or approximately twenty years of work.

a. Although every Christian has been given an equal amount of grace for salvation, what do we learn about what each has been given for service in the kingdom?

b. Jesus's hearers were to understand the great privilege of kingdom work. What more does Ephesians 2:10 teach us about the work that any Christian does in the service of the Lord?

c. There are several lists of gifts, abilities, opportunities, and so on throughout the New Testament, always with an emphasis on the *reason* they were given by God. According to Romans 12:4–8, 1 Corinthians 12:4–7, and 1 Peter 4:10–11, what are some of the reasons the different gifts have been given?

2. The grace of the master's actions is demonstrated by his trust of his own property to the servants. The Lord involves his people by allowing them to take what is precious to Him and multiply it in the world; it is the currency of the kingdom. To enter into the kingdom is to accept a responsibility. This is both a comfort and a challenge for the people of God.

   Along with each of the following challenges, what is the comfort the Lord gives, and how has he done that personally in your life?

   a. John 15:20

   b. Romans 12:9–14

   c. 2 Timothy 2:22–26

3. When the master returns, he evaluates the servants in the parable based on what they have done with what they had been given. As Frederick Bruner says, "Whatever the Lord gives now he will ask about later."[19]

a. What do you notice about the response of the master to the first two servants in verses 21 and 23?

b. What do the master's responses teach us about what characterizes life in the New Creation, when Jesus comes to bring in the fullness of the kingdom and final restoration of *all things*?

---

[19] Frederick Dale Bruner, *Matthew: A Commentary Vol. 1,* (Grand Rapids, MI: Eerdmans, 2004), 554.

c. How do the master's responses to the first two servants invalidate the third servant's assessment of the master?

4. There was a disconnect between the reality of who the master actually was and who the third servant perceived him to be. Jesus is affirming a principle that he has stressed throughout his training of the disciples: the importance of their careful and accurate conclusions regarding him. In each of the following passages, how does he patiently expand their awareness?

a. Matthew 16:13–19

b. John 1:47–51

   c. John 11:21–27

   d. John 14:8–11

5. What are some of the correctives or enlargements that Jesus has brought to your own perceptions of him as you have studied his kingdom parables?

6. There is an echo of Eden in the third servant's attitude toward the master. Sinful, guilty hearts can easily assume wicked and inaccurate thoughts about God. Read Genesis 3:8–12.

   a. What similarities and differences do you see in the servant's attitude and actions with those of Adam?

b. What are some misconceptions about God that Christians sometimes use to justify our actions or lack of them?

c. The parable illustrates a contrast between servants who know the Lord and desire to please him and a servant who does not know the Lord and has an unwarranted, servile fear of Him. This kind of fear is attended by wicked thoughts and actions. According to the following passages, what accompanies the believer's reverent, relational fear of the Lord, and how does each comfort you today?

Nehemiah 1:11

Psalm 86:11

Closing Thoughts

From the beginning chapters of Genesis, the biblical story paints a picture of a community of people who will function in the world using their gifts, abilities, talents, and knowledge for the glory of God. From the very first commands God gave to his human creatures, he made it clear that there is a principle of multiplication within their responsibility. God's kingdom was always intended to be *enlarged* by the faithful work of his people. The mandate to Adam, to Noah, to the Israelites, to the exiles in Babylon, to Christians today has never been repealed. God's people are to take the grace he has given and multiply it for his glory. He has already come and inaugurated his kingdom. He is coming again to collect his reward, the kingdom, which has been *expanded* to all the ends of the earth by his people through his Spirit.

There is one reason for our Lord's delay—the church still has much missional work to do! The kingdom resources must be invested and multiplied by the servants of the Lord until all the work has been done. The parable of the talents is a reminder to all Christians that we are not here to be bystanders in the story but to take our place and do the kingdom work that he has left us with all the resources he has given us.

Lesson 12

The Great Banquet

• • • • •

Read carefully Luke 14:1–24.

The parable of the great banquet is part of the narrative unit that is Luke 14. Jesus's teaching begins here with the issue of the social hierarchy of the times and then broadens out into the free offer of the gospel. The story belongs to a section some scholars have called "party parables." Some of Jesus's most pointed instructions and prophecies were communicated in social settings, particularly around the meal table. The discussion here at a dinner party becomes the launchpad for the very significant subject matter of who will and will not be present in the kingdom of God. What begins as a conversation on social etiquette and seating arrangements turns out to be much more far-reaching, consequential, and as usual, unexpected.

1. In this scene, Jesus is dining with a group of the socially elite, in the home of a ruler of the Pharisees. In an "after-dinner speech," the Lord deconstructs

everything the Pharisees think about meal invitation etiquette.

a. In Luke 14:12–14, to whom is Jesus speaking, and what are his puzzling instructions?

b. In verse 15, what was the immediate response of one of the guests, and according to John 8:33, what was most likely his presumption?

2. The practice in antiquity was to issue double invitations to a feast or banquet. After the first invitation went out and was accepted, the master could make preparations with full knowledge of how much food was necessary. Once the meal was ready, the final summons went out for the guests to come immediately. The assumption was that all who had responded yes would indeed

attend. It would have been a terrible defamation of the host to then refuse to come.

a. What were the excuses of the three, and what did each represent about different preoccupations of life?

b. According to Luke 14:25–33, what are the conditions of true discipleship to Jesus?

c. Every second of every day the Lord himself is inviting us to joyously feast with Him. Knowing that the preoccupations of life tend to get prioritized over spending time just enjoying Jesus's presence, what might be some ways we can reorder our days and intentionally seek him?

3. Invitations to meals or banquets in antiquity always signaled a line of demarcation between social insiders and outcasts. The master immediately instructs the servant to go and replace those who refused the invitation with those who were on the opposite end of the social spectrum.

a. Where is the servant told to go to issue that second round of invitations and to whom?

b. In preparation for the parable, what was the initial point Jesus had made in verses 12–14 regarding reciprocity? In what way would this point not only have shocked his hearers but been true of all these new invitees in his story?

c. What is the reason the master gives for the third round of invitations to be issued?

4. Jesus engages his listeners' imaginations in order to communicate difficult truths about who will and will not be at the kingdom feast, which has *already* begun with his first coming but will culminate with his second coming.

a. According to Romans 10:20–21, how does Paul then take those truths and convey them pointedly and directly?

b. From the beginning of Israel's existence, the Lord had persistently sought to gather his people in to be with him, and they had continually rejected that invitation. What has always been the poignant emotional response of God to that rejection?

Jeremiah 3:19.

Luke 13:33–34.

c. To what extent do you imitate the Lord's disposition of love and lament for the lost and rebellious in your family, community, or nation, and what are some ways you are demonstrating it to them? If you are not, how might you begin to cultivate that disposition?

5. In a similar but separate parable in Matthew 22, Jesus tells of another great feast given by a king—a wedding feast for his son.

    a. Read Matthew 22:11–14 with Luke 14:24. The Matthew passage relates an additional criterion for admission to the feast. What is required of those who will be in attendance at the wedding banquet of the king's son in the Matthew parable?

    b. Read Zechariah 3:1–5 with Revelation 7:9–12. Throughout the biblical story, what happens when God himself furnishes a person's clean garments?

    c. Read Revelation 19:6–9. Placing yourself joyfully in this future and certain scene, write down any thoughts of gratitude, joy, delight, majesty, triumph, resplendent beauty, or any other glorious, exalted reflections that this passage brings to your mind.

6. Christians cannot just be people who are *against* the things that exclude people from the kingdom of God. Christians must be people who have a vigorous and energetic compulsion to bring in the multitudes to the Great Banquet of the Lord Jesus Christ not just by talking about their faith in Jesus but by demonstrating that faith to a watching world. When you carefully examine your life, what about it is attractive and compelling to the unbeliever? What would cause him or her to say, "I want whatever it is that gives you such peace, love, joy, and faith"?

Closing Thoughts

The Jewish leaders rejected Christ because they drew the wrong conclusions regarding the purposes and promises of God for ethnic Israel. They could not see that the great feasting they were looking forward to participating in when God brought his promised kingdom had already begun with the coming of Jesus of Nazareth. They refused to come to the feast by way of the only invitation God had provided, through faith in his Son, even though they had been told in the parable that the feast is ready *now*. But the good news of the gospel is that God *will* have a people for himself, and the feast both now and in the New Creation will be attended by enormous numbers of jubilant partakers who have called on the name of Jesus for their eternal salvation. How amazing is the good news of the gospel of grace that includes all who will say yes to the feast! How it fills his people with joy to be numbered in that throng! How will you take what you have learned from the parables of Jesus and pursue those who are still outside of his kingdom with the incomparable offer of the eternal life he is offering them?

Bibliography

• • • • •

Blomberg, Craig L. *Contagious Holiness: Jesus' Meals with Sinners*. New Studies in Biblical Theology 19. Leicester, England: Downers Grove, IL: Apollos, InterVarsity Press, 2005.

Bruner, Frederick Dale. *Matthew: A Commentary Vol. 1*. Grand Rapids, MI: Eerdmans, 2004.

Edwards, James R. *The Gospel According to Luke. The Pillar New Testament Commentary*. D.A. Carson, General Ed. Grand Rapids, MI, 2015.

France, R.T. *The Gospel of Matthew. New International Commentary on the New Testament*. Ned B. Stonehouse, F.F. Bruce, and Gordon D. Fee, General Editors.

Grand Rapids, MI, 2007.

Green, Joel B. *The Gospel of Luke*. Grand Rapids, MI: Wm. B. Eerdmans Publishing Co., 1997.

Jones, Peter Rhea. *Studying the Parables of Jesus*. Macon, GA: Smyth & Helwys, 1999.

Keener, Craig S. *A Commentary on the Gospel of Matthew.* Grand Rapids, MI: W. B. Eerdmans Pub, 1999.

Kistemaker, Simon. *The Parables: Understanding the Stories Jesus Told.* New paperback ed. Grand Rapids, MI: Baker Books, 2002.

Morris, Leon. *The Gospel According to Matthew.* Grand Rapids, MI: Wm. B. Eerdmanns Publishing Co., 1992.

Snodgrass, Klyne. *Stories with Intent: A Comprehensive Guide to the Parables of Jesus.* Second edition. Grand Rapids, MI: William B. Eerdmans Publishing Company, 2018.

Wilkens, Steve, and Mark L. Sanford. *Hidden Worldviews: Eight Cultural Stories that Shape Our Lives.* Downers Grove, IL: IVP Academic, 2009.

Printed in the United States
by Baker & Taylor Publisher Services